4/06

THE SOLAR SYSTEM

MERCURY

A MyReportLinks.com Book

KIM A. O'CONNELL

MyReportLinks.com Books

an imprint of

 Enslow Publishers, Inc.

Box 398, 40 Industrial Road
Berkeley Heights, NJ 07922
USA

MyReportLinks.com Books, an imprint of Enslow Publishers, Inc. MyReportLinks®
is a registered trademark of Enslow Publishers, Inc.

Library of Congress Cataloging-in-Publication Data

O'Connell, Kim A.
  Mercury / Kim A. O'Connell.
    p. cm. — (The solar system)
  Includes bibliographical references and index.
  ISBN 0-7660-5209-5
  1. Mercury (Planet)—Juvenile literature. I. Title. II. Solar system (Berkeley Heights, N.J.)
  QB611.O26 2005
  523.41—dc22

                                    2004017793

Printed in the United States of America

10 9 8 7 6 5 4 3 2 1

To Our Readers:
Through the purchase of this book, you and your library gain access to the Report Links that specifically back
up this book.
The Publisher will provide access to the Report Links that back up this book and will keep these Report Links
up to date on **www.myreportlinks.com** for five years from the book's first publication date.
We have done our best to make sure all Internet addresses in this book were active and appropriate when we went
to press. However, the author and the Publisher have no control over, and assume no liability for, the material
available on those Internet sites or on other Web sites they may link to.
The usage of the MyReportLinks.com Books Web site is subject to the terms and conditions stated on the Usage
Policy Statement on **www.myreportlinks.com**.
A password may be required to access the Report Links that back up this book. The password is found on the
bottom of page 4 of this book.
Any comments or suggestions can be sent by e-mail to comments@myreportlinks.com or to the address on the
back cover.

Photo Credits: © Windows to the Universe, p. 10; European Space Agency, pp. 42, 44; Lunar and Planetary
Institute, pp. 12, 18, 23, 25; MyReportLinks.com Books, p. 4; NASA, pp. 17, 27, 36, 43; NASA/Jet Propulsion
Laboratory, pp. 16, 20, 29, 31, 33, 38, 39; NASA/Jet Propulsion Laboratory/Northwestern University, p. 22;
NASA/Johns Hopkins University Applied Physics Laboratory/Carnegie Institute of Washington, pp. 13, 41;
United States Geological Survey, pp. 1, 3, 9; University of St. Andrews, p. 26.

Note: Some NASA photos were only available in a low-resolution format.

Cover Photo: Orthographic map of Mercury, centered at its equator; United States Geological Survey.

Report Links 4

Mercury Facts 9

1 ▶ **Mercury the Messenger** 10

2 ▶ **The First Planet From the Sun** 15

3 ▶ **Rotations and Revolutions** 24

4 ▶ **Special Features** 29

5 ▶ **Exploring Mercury** 35

Glossary 45

Chapter Notes 46

Further Reading 47

Index 48

About MyReportLinks.com Books

MyReportLinks.com Books
Great Books, Great Links, Great for Research!

The Internet sites listed on the next four pages can save you hours of research time. These Internet sites—we call them "Report Links"—are constantly changing, but we keep them up to date on our Web site.

Give it a try! Type http://www.myreportlinks.com into your browser, click on the series title, then the book title, and scroll down to the Report Links listed for this book.

The Report Links will bring you to great source documents, photographs, and illustrations. MyReportLinks.com Books save you time, feature Report Links that are kept up to date, and make report writing easier than ever!

Please see "To Our Readers" on the copyright page for important information about this book, the MyReportLinks.com Web site, and the Report Links that back up this book.

Please enter **PME1743** if asked for a password.

Report Links

 The Internet sites described below can be accessed at
http://www.myreportlinks.com

*EDITOR'S CHOICE

▶**Mercury: Your Travel Guide to the Solar System**
Journey with the BBC to the planet Mercury through text, images,
and video. This site gives basic facts and highlights major surface features
of the closest planet to the Sun.

*EDITOR'S CHOICE

▶**Planetary Photojournal: Mercury**
View sixty-four NASA photographs of Mercury taken by the *Mariner 10*
spacecraft, currently the only spacecraft to visit Mercury. Each image
has an explanatory caption.

*EDITOR'S CHOICE

▶*Messenger*
The official Web site of NASA's *Messenger* mission offers information on
the first mission to Mercury since *Mariner 10*. Build your own model of
the *Messenger* spacecraft from downloadable plans.

*EDITOR'S CHOICE

▶**Solar System Exploration: Mercury**
This NASA site offers a profile of Mercury and provides links to more
information about the first planet from the Sun.

*EDITOR'S CHOICE

▶**Exploring the Planets: Mercury**
This Web site from the Smithsonian's National Air and Space Museum
provides facts and images of Mercury.

*EDITOR'S CHOICE

▶**Mercury**
This NASA site has several Mercury resources, including a book list,
mission summaries, and a discussion of the evidence for ice on Mercury.
Mariner's images of Mercury are included.

Report Links

The Internet sites described below can be accessed at http://www.myreportlinks.com

▶ Ask an Astronomer for Kids!: Mercury

From the California Institute of Technology comes a site that offers simple answers to kids' questions about Mercury. It also offers the chance to ask an astronomer a new question and get answers about other planets.

▶ Astronomy: Planets—Mercury

Sponsored by the Institute of Physics, this site lists statistics for Mercury's surface characteristics, orbit, magnetic field, atmosphere, and appearance from Earth.

▶ Atlas of Mercury

This NASA site presents more than a hundred Mercury images, plus basic facts, ancient mythology, and a detailed description of exploration and mapping efforts.

▶ BepiColombo

The European Space Agency (ESA) and Japan's space agency are teaming up on a Mercury mission named for a leading Italian scientist. Read about this mission's goals at the ESA site.

▶ Cape Canaveral Air Force Station

Cape Canaveral, Florida, is the site where NASA's *Messenger* mission to Mercury was launched in 2004. This Web site provides a history of space launches at Cape Canaveral and information about current activities.

▶ Edmond Halley

From the University of St. Andrews, Scotland, comes a biography of Edmond Halley, the first man to observe a full Mercury transit.

▶ Edmond Halley (October 29, 1656–January 14, 1742)

A biography of Edmond Halley, who first witnessed a transit of Mercury, is offered by the Students for the Exploration and Development of Space Web site. Halley used transits to come up with a more accurate measurement of the planets in the solar system.

▶ Exploring Planets in the Classroom

Let the people at Hawaii's Space Grant College show you how to make impact craters like the ones on Mercury and the Moon. Hands-on activities are offered at this site.

Report Links

**The Internet sites described below can be accessed at
http://www.myreportlinks.com**

▶**Hermes**

On this Web site read about Hermes, the messenger god in Greek mythology who was the Roman god Mercury's counterpart.

▶**IAU Rules and Conventions**

The International Astronomical Union is the organization responsible for assigning names to astronomical bodies and their surface features, such as the surface features on Mercury and other planets. Learn more about this group's work at this Web site.

▶**Journey to the Planets and Beyond**

NASA's Jet Propulsion Laboratory (JPL) has been making discoveries about Mercury and other worlds for over forty years. This site offers a time line of the missions that JPL has been a part of.

▶**Mercury: Closest Planet to the Sun**

This Planetary Society Web site has a chart that compares Mercury's features with those of Earth and the Moon. Some of the items compared are size, mass, gravity, and temperature.

▶**Mercury: Planetary Geology of an Enigmatic Neighbour**

The Royal Astronomical Society of Canada Web page on Mercury focuses on the geology of the half of Mercury mapped by *Mariner 10*. The site also includes diagrams of Mercury's interior.

▶**Mercury *Mariner 10* Image Project**

An archive of Mercury images taken by *Mariner 10* is offered at this Northwestern University site. Also included are original mission bulletins, which highlight the difficulties of space exploration.

▶**Mercury Nomenclature Table of Contents**

This United States Geological Survey site presents locations and descriptions of all named features of the planet Mercury. Included with each feature is an explanation of how it got its name.

▶**New Data, New Ideas, and Lively Debate About Mercury**

At this site, see how scientists are reworking and integrating *Mariner 10* data with more recent Earth-based measurements to learn new things about Mercury.

Report Links

**The Internet sites described below can be accessed at
http://www.myreportlinks.com**

▶**The Nine Planets: Mercury**

Mercury is the closest planet to the Sun and is smaller than every planet but Pluto.
Read more about Mercury on this Web site.

▶**The Planet Mercury: It's Hot, Heavy, and Inhospitable**

From the editors of *Space Today* comes a site with detailed information about Mercury
and its environment. Current and future exploration efforts are included.

▶**Solar System Formation**

This University of Colorado site examines the current theories that explain how
Mercury and the other planets in the solar system came to be.

▶**Space Educators' Handbook: Mercury**

The NASA Space Educators' Handbook site offers two dozen "quick facts" about
Mercury. Reference sources are included.

▶**StarDate Online: Mercury**

This observatory's site on Mercury presents basic facts and links to more than sixty
audio stories about the planet. Hints for finding Mercury in the sky are included.

▶**Thomas Harriot**

This Scottish university Web site offers a biography of the English astronomer Thomas
Harriot, who worked at the same time that Galileo did.

▶**The Voyage of *Mariner 10*—Mission to Venus and Mercury**

Read the official NASA history of *Mariner 10,* so far the only spacecraft to explore
Mercury. This site covers the mission and the people who made it possible.

▶**Windows to the Universe: Mercury**

This university Web site offers a great deal of information about Mercury, including how
it got its name, as well as photos of the planet.

Mercury Facts

Age
About 4.5 billion years

Diameter at Equator
3,032 miles (4,878 kilometers)

Composition
Core of iron and nickel; rocky mantle; thin crust

Average Distance From the Sun
About 36 million miles (58 million kilometers)

Orbital Period (year, in Earth days)
87.9 Earth days

Rotational Period (day, in Earth days)
174 Earth days

Duration of One Day (sunrise to sunset)
58.6 Earth days

Mass
5.5 percent of Earth's mass

Temperature
Up to 872°F (467ºC) at surface. Nighttime temperatures
of −279°F (−173°C)

Surface Gravity
39 percent of Earth's gravity (If you weighed 100 pounds on Earth,
you would weigh 39 pounds on Mercury.)

Mercury the Messenger

In the ancient world, people noticed a faint "star" in the sky that behaved differently than others. Instead of holding a position in a familiar grouping of stars known as a constellation, this star seemed to follow the Sun as it rose and set each day. Later, the ancient Greeks and other civilizations recognized that this star was actually a planet, one of several known to the ancients. Because this planet moved more quickly than others, the Greeks

Image: "Mercury and Argos" by Velazquez.
courtesy of the Museo Nacional del Prado, Madrid, Spain.

▲ The figure on the right of this painting depicts Mercury, the Roman god of transportation and commerce and the namesake of the first planet in our solar system. Mercury served as a messenger to the other gods.

named it Hermes, after the swift messenger of the gods in Greek mythology. The ancient Egyptian and Maya civilizations also thought that this fast-moving planet was similar to the messengers in their origin legends. The Romans eventually followed suit, naming the planet Mercury after their own mythological messenger. The Roman name of this small, mysterious planet is the name that we continue to use today.

In the early 1600s, astronomers including the famous Italian Galileo Galilei and the less-well-known Englishman Thomas Harriot began using telescopes to view objects in the sky and record their observations. From the beginning, it was nearly impossible to make out details about Mercury, which always swung close to the blinding Sun. Eventually, astronomers were able to use larger and stronger telescopes to study this planet and others. By the late 1700s, astronomers were drawing crude maps of the dark blotches on Mercury's surface. By the 1880s, two astronomers, Giovanni Schiaparelli and William Denning, recorded their observations of Mercury on maps to identify landmarks that would move due to the planet's rotation. (Neither astronomer correctly calculated the length of time it took Mercury to rotate, however.)

It was not until nearly a century later, in the mid-1970s, that the National Aeronautics and Space Administration, NASA, launched an unmanned space probe named *Mariner 10,* which made three flybys of the planet and captured thousands of images of Mercury. Those images, as valuable as they are, only covered about half of the planet's surface. Today, even though we know much more about Mercury than we did just thirty years ago, the first planet from the Sun remains one of the least-studied planets in our solar system.

▷ Small, Hot, and Speedy

As the closest planet to the Sun, Mercury features a surface that is extremely hot, with temperatures reaching 872°F (467°C). Only Venus, with its dense atmosphere holding in heat, is hotter.

▲ *Mercury is the smallest of the four terrestrial planets (shown here) and the second smallest planet in the solar system after Pluto.*

Mercury is also a small planet, with a diameter of only 3,032 miles (4,878 kilometers)—just over a third of Earth's diameter and smaller even than some of the moons of Jupiter and Saturn. Mercury may be small, but what it lacks in size it makes up for in speed. Orbiting the Sun like a rocket, Mercury moves at a rate of up to 35 miles per second (56.3 kilometers per second)—the fastest moving planet in the solar system.

Mercury looks a lot like another celestial body: Earth's Moon. Mercury is only 40 percent larger than the Moon, and the planet's copper-colored surface is marked by craters found among highlands and lowland plains. Like the Moon, Mercury has barely any atmosphere. Mercury is also a relatively dense planet, made up of about 70 percent iron. Because Mercury lacks the basic elements that cause major surface changes—including air, water, and major volcanic activity—some scientists consider Mercury to be a planetary fossil. As far as we know, the planet has not changed much in several billion years.

▶ Messenger's Mission

Soon, some of Mercury's secrets may be uncovered. On August 3, 2004, NASA's *Messenger* spacecraft was launched aboard a Delta 2 rocket from Cape Canaveral, Florida, into the early morning sky.

The unmanned probe began a 5-billion-mile (8-billion-kilometer), seven-year journey to Mercury. The mission's name, a nod to the mythological figure for whom the planet is named, combines the first letters of a phrase describing the mission itself: MErcury Surface, Space ENvironment, GEochemistry, and Ranging. If successful, *Messenger* will enter Mercury's orbit in 2011, after getting a little "boost" from some other planets. In part because of the

▲ *This artist's picture shows the unmanned* Messenger *spacecraft approaching Mercury. Although the probe was launched in August 2004, it is not expected to reach the planet until March 2011.*

weight of the craft itself (heavy with fuel) and the relatively small size of the rocket powering it, *Messenger* will need gravity assists. In a mechanism something like a slingshot, *Messenger* will first get a boost from Earth's gravity, which will propel it toward Venus. Then Venus, in turn, will propel the probe toward Mercury. Mercury's gravity will capture the probe during its third flyby of the planet.[1]

The spacecraft is equipped with seven instruments to study Mercury's entire surface as well as its core, its atmosphere, and its magnetic field, all for the first time. Some of those instruments will measure how solar X-rays interact with Mercury's surface. By measuring these X-rays, scientists should be able to determine the kinds of elements that can be found in the planet's crust. By studying the data, scientists can learn more about how Mercury was formed.

"For nearly thirty years, we've had questions that couldn't be answered until technology and mission designs caught up with our desire to go back to Mercury," said Dr. Sean Solomon, an investigator with the *Messenger* mission. "Now we are ready. The answers to these questions will not only tell us more about Mercury, but illuminate processes that affect all the terrestrial planets."[2]

Chapter 2

The First Planet From the Sun

Without the aid of satellites, computers, or even telescopes, most people in ancient civilizations believed that an unmoving Earth was at the center of the universe. After all, people on Earth could not see that it moved, but they could see that other celestial bodies moved from place to place in the sky. Eventually, by observing and understanding the movements of planets, people came to understand that Earth, like the other known planets, orbited the Sun in a group of planets, stars, asteroids, comets, and other bodies known as the solar system. But this understanding did not arrive quickly or easily.

▶ Early Astronomy

Although the ancient Greeks came to believe that Earth was round rather than flat, most of them continued to believe that the Sun revolved around Earth. A second-century A.D. Greek philosopher named Ptolemy helped to cement that view, which continued for a long time. The idea of an Earth-centered universe went mostly unchallenged until the sixteenth century. In 1543, the Polish astronomer Nicolaus Copernicus was able to argue convincingly that Earth, a planet like Mercury, Venus, Mars, and Jupiter (the other known planets at the time), revolved around a stationary Sun. His ideas, revolutionary for the time, were reinforced in the 1600s by Johannes Kepler, a German astronomer who also discovered that the planets moved in an elliptical orbit around the Sun rather than a circular one. With the invention of the telescope, astronomers began to learn more about the bodies

▲ *The* Mariner 10 *spacecraft photographed this illuminated hemisphere of Mercury after passing the dark side of the planet.*

in our solar system, although much remained unclear until the birth of spaceflight in the mid-twentieth century.

The Birth of the Solar System

Most astronomers believe that the solar system began in an enormous cloud of gas and dust, more than 4 billion years ago. Eventually, the cloud collapsed and compressed, forming a heated core with a disk of dust, gas, and rocks circling around it. Over millions of years, these particles began to stick together. As these clumps grew, they pulled in other particles, forming the beginnings of planets. These early planetary orbs continually collided with each other, with larger planets absorbing smaller ones.

▲ *Mercury was one of the planets known to the ancients. Here, Mercury and other planets gather over Stonehenge, a famous standing-stone monument built by prehistoric people in what is now southern England.*

The gravitational pull of some planets drew in clouds of interstellar gas—creating Saturn, Uranus, Neptune, and Pluto, the outer planets, known as gas giants. Others—like Mercury, Mars, Earth, and Venus, the inner planets, closest to the Sun— remained primarily rocky. These planets are known as terrestrial planets because they have solid rocky surfaces. (*Terrestrial* refers to something that is like Earth.) Mercury and Venus are similar in that they are the only planets that do not have moons (also called satellites). Mercury and Earth, however, are very different from each other.

▷ A Core of Iron

Most scientists think that Mercury formed out of a series of collisions with other rocky matter in the cluttered period when the solar system was forming. Another theory proposes that Mercury

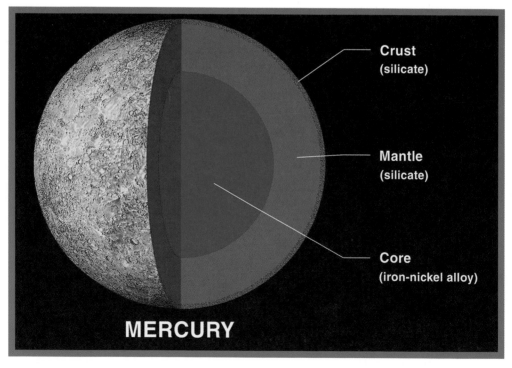

▲ *Mercury is like Earth in that it has a core, mantle, and crust. But scientists think that Mercury's core is much larger relative to the planet's size.*

might have been created deeper into the solar system but that a collision knocked the young planet toward the Sun and into its current orbit. Mercury also probably began its existence spinning much faster than it does now. Although the reasons for the "spin down" are not entirely clear, most scientists agree that the Sun exerts a strong force on the planet, pulling on it in an endless game of galactic tug-of-war. As a result, Mercury, a fast-moving planet, has the second-slowest rotation period in the entire solar system—taking 58.65 days to turn on its axis. Only Venus spins more slowly.

Like the other terrestrial planets, Mercury is a dense ball of rock and iron—the second-densest planet in the solar system after Earth. Yet Mercury's iron content has turned out to be much higher than scientists first expected. The planet is thought to be about 70 percent iron (with some nickel) and 30 percent silicate. Large planets tend to be dense because their great outer mass condenses the inner core. But this is less likely to be the reason that a small planet like Mercury is so dense. Some say that, in its earliest form, Mercury might have been covered with a thick, rocky mantle, or outer layer. A later collision might have stripped away most of this rocky layer, leaving only a dense, iron-rich "dwarf planet" with a very thin crust. Mercury's iron content is concentrated in an almost completely solid core, which extends about three quarters of the way from the center of the planet to its outer crust.

Because of the iron core, which may be partly molten, Mercury, like Earth, has a magnetic field, which is an area of magnetic energy around the planet. That field was first discovered on the *Mariner 10* mission. Mercury's magnetic field is much less strong than Earth's, though. The only other planets with measurable magnetic fields are Jupiter, Saturn, Neptune, and Uranus.

Size and Surface

Mercury is the second-smallest planet in the solar system after Pluto. It would take three planets of Mercury's size to equal just

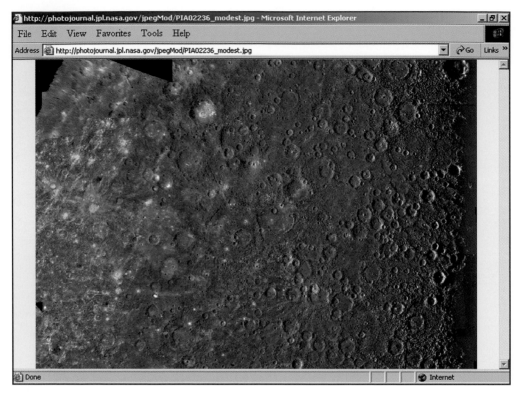

▲ *This image taken by* Mariner 10 *of the Kuiper Quadrangle shows some of the many craters on Mercury's surface.*

one Earth. For centuries, astronomers, including even those as prominent as Galileo, could not figure out how large Mercury was. Telescopes did not become strong enough to take really accurate measurements until the 1700s. Then, astronomers theorized that the planet's diameter ranged from between 2,700 and 4,000 miles (4,300 and 6,500 kilometers), which made Mercury the smallest planet ever discovered. Mercury was considered the smallest planet in the solar system until 1980, when scientists determined that Pluto was less than half the size of Mercury.

▶ The Craters of Mercury

At first glance, Mercury's crater-pocked surface looks very similar to the surface of Earth's Moon. Looking more closely, however, key differences are visible. Mercury's craters are less densely packed than the Moon's. This finding surprised early researchers. Eventually, observers came to believe that a major event in Mercury's history covered over most of the planet's earliest impact craters—craters formed not from volcanic eruption but from the bombardment of objects such as meteors, asteroids, and comets over billions of years. Evidence for this theory exists in the large, gently rolling plains that can be found between the heavily cratered sections. These plains are covered with much smaller craters that formed from more recent impacts. Mercury's surface also features long cliffs that wind and bend across the planet's surface for hundreds of miles.

Craters on Mercury come in all shapes and sizes. Small craters are shaped like cereal bowls. The larger the crater, the flatter its bottom. In addition, material ejected from the craters—called "ejecta blankets"—have different proportions than those on the Moon. Ejecta blankets look like halos or rays around craters. Because Mercury's gravitational pull is almost twice as strong as the Moon's, material falls to the surface more quickly on Mercury. In other words, if impacts created two craters of the exact same diameter on the surfaces of Mercury and the Moon, the debris ejected out of the basins would fall only half as far on Mercury as it would on the Moon.

When viewing photos of Mercury's surface, it is easy to tell the older craters from the younger ones. Young craters have sharp edges and bright, easily visible ejecta blankets. The edges of older craters are usually softer than those of younger craters, and their rims have been worn down by younger, smaller craters and impact marks.

Hot and Cold Extremes

Because Mercury is so close to the Sun, its surface temperatures can reach more than 800°F (427°C). The planet has almost no atmosphere, although it does occasionally capture hydrogen or helium gas given off by the Sun. Without any atmosphere to trap heat, surface temperatures can also drop to −300°F (−184°C) or even colder. Mercury has the greatest range of temperatures of any planet. This is partly caused by Mercury's long day. On Mercury, the period from sunrise to sunset lasts about three Earth months, which gives the surface in the daylight plenty of time to heat up. On the other side of the planet, Mercury's nighttime lasts just as long, a good long time for a freeze. Scientists are pretty certain that ice can even be found in some of the deepest craters at the poles, whose corners and nooks never see the Sun.

A planet's internal temperature is also important. The hotter a planet's interior, the more active its surface tends to be. Earth has maintained a high internal temperature throughout its life.

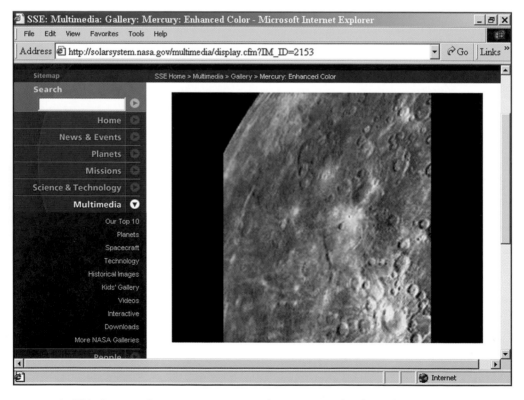

▲ This image of Mercury was created using special color enhancement. The addition of color helps scientists identify those materials that make up the planet's surface and determine its age and iron content.

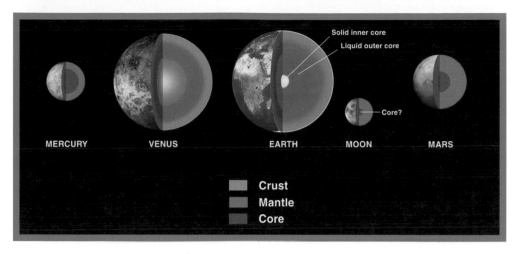

Solid inner core
Liquid outer core

MERCURY   VENUS   EARTH   MOON   MARS

Core?

Crust
Mantle
Core

▲ *The structures of the terrestrial planets and Earth's Moon are compared in this diagram.*

As a result, it has volcanoes, earthquakes, and other geological events that shape and mold its surface. Scientists believe that Mercury was once blistering hot, covered with a molten liquid layer. As this layer cooled, Mercury condensed, and its diameter shrunk greatly. The planet became a dense, inactive planet, changing very little over the course of its more recent history.

"Mercury remains . . . a world of extreme contrasts and unexpected surprises," space scientist Faith Vilas has written. "Just when scientists believe they understand what is happening on and within it, innovative observations probe a little deeper into Mercury's secrets. And each new revelation seems more improbable than the last."[1]

Rotations and Revolutions

Even though Mercury is closer to the Sun than any other planet, it is still very far away—on average, 36 million miles (58 million kilometers) from our closest star. If you were able to stand on Mercury and see the Sun at its highest point in the sky, it would appear at least twice as large on Mercury as it does to us on Earth.

▶ Spin Cycles

We know that a day on Earth lasts twenty-four hours—the time it takes our planet to rotate once on its axis. A day on Mercury, however, is much longer: Mercury rotates on its axis once every 58.65 Earth days. Mercury's rotational period is the second slowest in the solar system.

Mercury's orbital period, the time that it takes to revolve around the Sun, is much faster than Earth's, however. While it takes one year, or 365 days, for Earth to revolve around the Sun, it takes Mercury only about 88 days to complete its orbit, because Mercury is the fastest moving planet in the solar system. It also has a shorter distance to travel around the Sun than Earth does.

Mercury also has the second-most elliptical orbit after Pluto. Mercury changes speed as it travels around the Sun, going faster when it nears the Sun and slower as it moves away. At its closest point to the Sun, Mercury travels at about 35 miles per second (56 kilometers per second), but at the planet's most distant point, it is traveling at about 24 miles per second (39 kilometers per second)—slower, but still incredibly fast in planetary terms. "If an airplane could travel at this speed," the planetary researcher

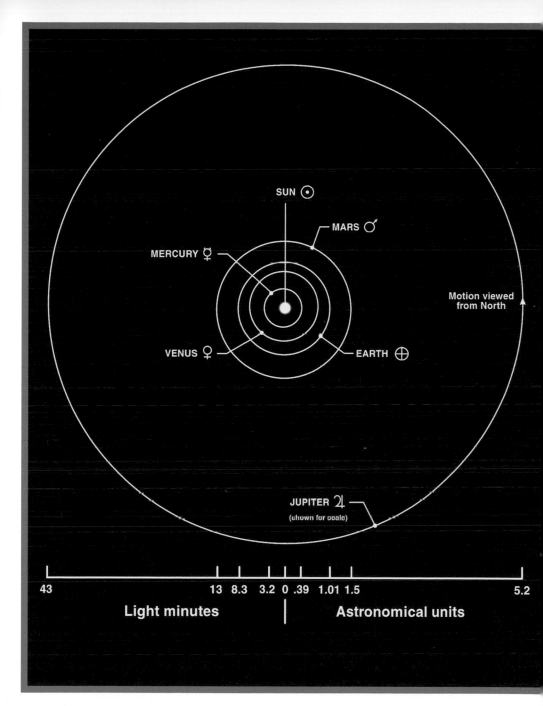

▲ This scaled diagram shows the approximate distances of the four terrestrial planets from the Sun. (Jupiter is added to give an idea of its distance from the terrestrial planets.)

Robert Strom has written, "it would take less than twelve minutes to circle the Earth."[1]

Mercury's rotational and orbital periods result in an interesting relationship. Mercury rotates exactly three times for every two orbits of the Sun. To astronomers, this ratio is known as a spin-orbit coupling. Because our own Moon rotates on its axis as it orbits Earth, it also has a spin-orbit coupling. The Moon makes both a complete rotation and a complete orbit in one lunar day.

Transits of the Sun

Every few years, Mercury offers observers on Earth a special treat—a transit across the Sun. A transit occurs when a planet passes between Earth and the Sun. During this event, the planet

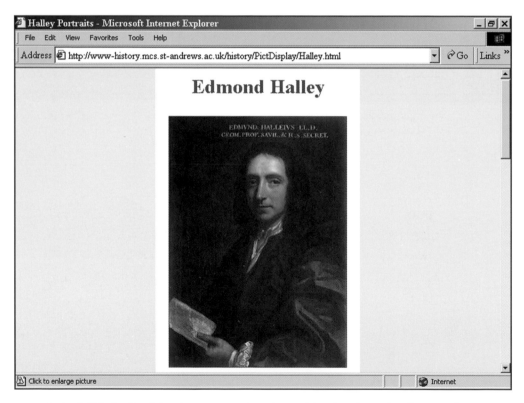

In 1677, the English astronomer and mathematician Sir Edmond Halley was the first to observe a transit of Mercury.

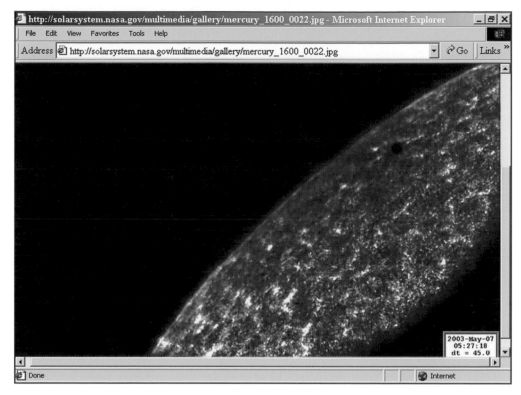

http://solarsystem.nasa.gov/multimedia/gallery/mercury_1600_0022.jpg - Microsoft Internet Explorer

File   Edit   View   Favorites   Tools   Help

Address http://solarsystem.nasa.gov/multimedia/gallery/mercury_1600_0022.jpg   Go   Links

2003-May-07
05:27:18
dt = 45.0

Done   Internet

▲ *The last transit of Mercury occurred on May 7, 2003. In this photograph, the planet appears as a black dot on the surface of the Sun.*

appears as a small dark disk against the Sun's bright orange ball. Transits are similar to solar eclipses in which the Moon passes between Earth and the Sun. Since Mercury and Venus are the only two planets between Earth and the Sun, they are the only planets whose transits are visible from Earth. Similarly, people on Earth can also see phases of Mercury and Venus as they orbit the Sun, just as we can see the phases of the Moon as it orbits Earth.

Transits were first used in the 1700s to help astronomers make accurate measurements of the distance between Earth and the Sun. Sir Edmond Halley, an English mathematician and astronomer, is well known as the first astronomer to accurately predict the return of a comet every seventy-six years. That comet, formerly known as the great comet of 1682, is now called Halley's comet, in his honor.

But Halley was also the first astronomer to figure out that by comparing transits and orbits, he could accurately measure the distance between Earth and the Sun, which led to an absolute scale of the solar system. In 1677, Halley became the first astronomer to observe a transit of Mercury while he was on a trip to St. Helena, an island in the South Atlantic, to catalog the stars of the Southern Hemisphere.

Viewing a Transit of Mercury

Mercury is so small that observers need a telescope to witness the planet's transit of the Sun. But a telescope needs to be outfitted with special filters to block out the Sun's harmful rays, since eye damage and even blindness can occur when looking at the Sun for only a few seconds. Transits of Mercury take place about once every seven years. The last transit of Mercury was in May 2003, the first of fourteen transits of the planet that will happen in the twenty-first century. The next transit of Mercury will be in November 2006.

Chapter 4 ▶

Special Features

In the 1970s, *Mariner 10* sent back thousands of images of Mercury's surface. These images have formed the basis of most of our understanding of the planet. Even with all this new information on the first planet from the Sun, *Mariner* photographed less than half of Mercury's surface. The *Messenger* mission should help to fill in the gaps in our knowledge of Mercury.

Still, Mercury has revealed enough information for us to know that it is divided into highland and lowland areas. The highlands are covered with craters and long ridges known as scarps, while the lowlands are notable for their large, smooth plains. Mercury's most famous lowland area is the Caloris Basin—a cratered portion of the planet that resulted from a massive collision billions of years ago.

Although it seems obvious to us now, astronomers did not agree on the origins of impact craters until the lunar missions of the 1960s. Some thought all craters were the result of volcanic

Mariner 10 *took this image of* ▶ Mercury's surface just after the spacecraft made its closest approach to the planet, on March 29, 1974.

eruptions, while others correctly believed they were the result of impacts caused by the bombardment of meteors. Such impacts have had a profound effect on Mercury's surface—in the form of craters, mountain ridges, and basins.

When a planet or other object reflects a lot of light and appears quite bright, its albedo, or reflective power, is high. Mercury has a low albedo when compared with the albedos of Venus, Earth, and Mars, the other terrestrial planets. In general, the less dense the atmosphere, the lower the planet's albedo, and the atmosphere of Mercury, if it can be said to have one, is very thin.

Highlands and Lowlands

Mercury is pocked with hundreds of craters, which are ringed with vast mountain ranges that form highlands. Unlike many of the Moon's craters, however, Mercury's widest craters are rather shallow. The spaces between these wide craters are known as the intercrater plains. These plains are fairly smooth although they do feature much smaller, oddly shaped craters. These secondary craters, caused by material ejected from other impacts elsewhere on the surface, are usually elongated and sometimes even open on one end.

The highlands, which cover about 70 percent of Mercury's surface, are the oldest visible part of the planet. They were probably created about 400 million years after the solar system was first formed. The intercrater plains, which are ancient lava flows, were formed more recently. The youngest visible features on Mercury are the lowlands, which are much larger, smoother sections of the planet than the highlands. Generally, these plains are located near Mercury's north pole and major impact areas, such as the large Caloris Basin.

Some of the strangest surface features that have been discovered on Mercury are its scarps. These long cliffs can run for more than 300 miles (483 kilometers) and reach up to 2.5 miles (4 kilometers) high. Scarps stretch across every feature in their

▲ *This image of Mercury was created by piecing together several images of the planet taken by* Mariner 10.

path, including craters and basins. Scientists believe that scarps are caused by compression in Mercury's crust. As the planet has cooled over time, its surface has contracted, cracking like a concrete sidewalk, with the scarps the edges of these cracks. No other planet features cliffs like these in such wide distribution.

What's in a Name?

The surface features on Mercury bear the names of famous people, places, and things. Craters have been named for the nineteenth-century novelist Charles Dickens, the great Italian Renaissance artist Michelangelo, and the famous German composer Beethoven. One crater has been named for Gerard P. Kuiper, a Dutch-American astronomer whom many consider to be the father of modern planetary science. (The Kuiper Belt, a vast ring of small icy bodies that orbit the Sun beyond Neptune, has also been named for this famous scientist.) The valleys on Mercury are named for prominent radio observatories—with names such as Arecibo and Goldstone—while the cliffs or scarps are named for astronomers and famous ships, such as *Victoria*.

The Caloris Basin

The most fascinating section of Mercury's surface is the Caloris Basin. This giant cratered section of the planet—about 800 miles (1,300 kilometers) in diameter—is the result of a massive collision that took place about 3.85 billion years ago. The basin's name comes from the Latin *calor*, which means "heat." The Caloris Basin lies near the planet's hottest point when it is closest to the Sun.

Scientists believe the impact that created this basin fueled massive seismic waves that shook the ground and affected the entire planet. The impact that created the Caloris Basin had the energy of about one trillion mega-hydrogen bombs, according to one estimate. "It was an event with global consequences for the

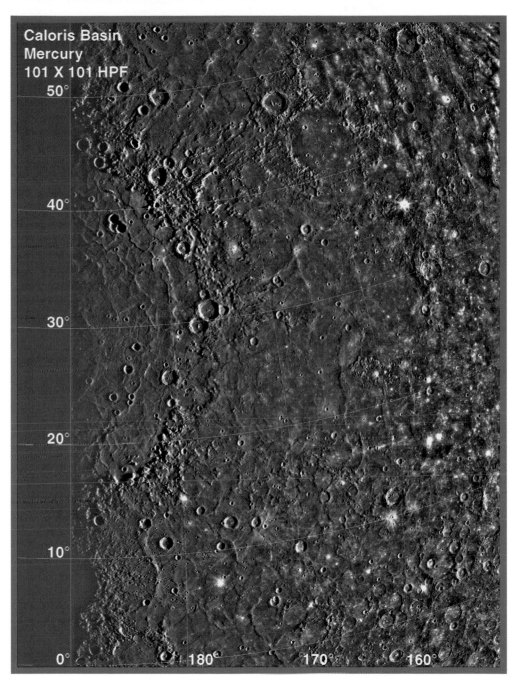

Caloris Basin
Mercury
101 X 101 HPF

▲ At 800 miles (1,300 kilometers) in diameter, the Caloris Basin (shown here) is the largest impact basin on Mercury and the second largest to be found on the terrestrial planets.

▶ 33 ◀

young planet," writes scientist Faith Vilas, "and its manifestations are not limited to the region around the basin."[1]

The Caloris Basin is the second-largest impact basin that has been discovered among the terrestrial planets—bigger than the entire state of Texas. (The Mare Orientale, about twice the diameter of the Caloris Basin, is found on the Moon's far side.) The edge of Caloris is a ring of broken mountain ranges, reaching about 1.25 miles (2 kilometers) high. The basin's floor is covered in smooth plains that are broken up by ridges and fractures. Radiating outward from the basin's center, like the spokes of a bicycle wheel, is the Van Eyck Formation, a series of long hilly ridges and grooves. Beyond this formation lie lower hills, which finally become rolling plains known as the Odin Formation.

Another interesting effect that has come from the formation of the Caloris Basin can be found on the exact opposite side of the impact point. As shock waves from the initial impact moved through the planet's core, they finally reached the opposite side, which caused the ground there to crack and push upward. The *Mariner 10* imaging team called this section Mercury's "weird terrain."[2]

Chapter 5

Exploring Mercury

Ever since the ancients spotted Mercury's unique position in relation to the Sun, observers have longed to learn more about this mysterious planet. In addition to seeking data about the planet itself, astronomers knew that Mercury might also offer information about the solar system as a whole. Mercury's surface also offers clues to the origins and early years of the planets—such as the period of heavy bombardment that left numerous craters on Mercury's landscape.

Throughout the nineteenth and early twentieth centuries, astronomers trained their telescopes on Mercury, drawing crude maps of the darker splotches that could be seen on the planet's surface. These maps, which often differed from one another, nevertheless formed the basis of all our astronomical understanding of Mercury until the early 1970s. Then, completely controlled from Earth, the unmanned *Mariner 10* space probe changed our view of Mercury forever.

▶ *Mariner 10*

In the early 1970s, NASA was facing budget cuts. To save money on planetary research, NASA decided to use a method known as a gravity assist to study both Venus and Mercury on a single mission. Like a rock from a slingshot, the *Mariner 10* spacecraft would first be propelled by Earth's gravity toward Venus, where it would be slowed by Venus's gravitational field. Then, it would be in a good position to rocket into a rendezvous with Mercury. Using this method, *Mariner 10* flew past Mercury three times: March 29 and September 21, 1974, and March 16, 1975.

▲ *An Atlas-Centaur rocket carrying* Mariner 10 *was launched from Cape Canaveral, Florida, on November 3, 1973.*

The mission's value to planetary researchers was enormous. The spacecraft sent back thousands of photographs. These photos enabled accurate maps of the planet to be created for the first time. In addition, *Mariner 10* took photos of Earth, and this marked the first time that our planet had been photographed from distances farther away than the Moon. The *Mariner 10* spacecraft was outfitted with the most advanced scientific instruments that had ever been developed. Special heat shields and solar panels protected the spacecraft from the extremely intense heat and radiation from the Sun. And an onboard computer could be monitored and programmed by NASA scientists on Earth.

Maneuvering *Mariner*

The first Mercury flyby was considered a success. It revealed Mercury's Moonlike cratered surface and allowed accurate measurements of the planet's mass and density. Yet NASA scientists still had to find a way to ensure the second and third flybys of the planet.

By the second flyby, *Mariner 10* was experiencing critical problems. The temperature in the electronics department rose unexpectedly, and power began to drain from the spacecraft. By turning some systems off and reprogramming the craft, NASA engineers managed to keep *Mariner* going long enough to complete the mission. During this flyby, the craft photographed the planet's southern hemisphere and took photos of previously seen areas from different angles.

By the third trip, however, *Mariner* was running dangerously low on the propellant required to keep it in the correct position—or attitude—for the mission. At one point, the spacecraft rolled upside down, breaking off computer communications with Earth. After some emergency meetings, NASA scientists figured out how to use a powerful antenna on Earth to send a signal to the ship and reprogram it into the correct position. Once it was righted, the ship sent back high-resolution photographs of the planet's surface and measured the planet's magnetic field.

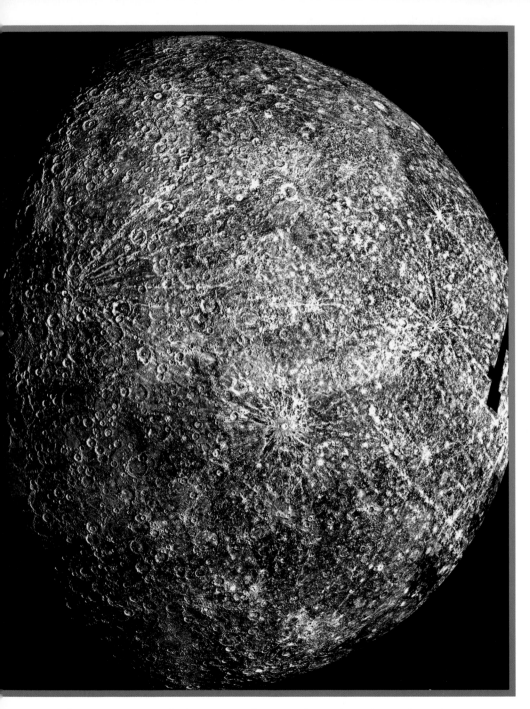

▲ Mariner 10 *took this image of Mercury's southern hemisphere during its second flyby of the planet.*

Finally, on March 24, 1975, the *Mariner 10* spacecraft ran out of the propellant that controlled its position. This sent the spacecraft into an uncontrollable spin—and broke off all communications with Earth for good. Today, *Mariner 10* is still spinning in space, locked in an endless orbit around the Sun.

▷ Polar Ice Caps—on Mercury?

Following *Mariner 10*'s successful mission in the 1970s, scientists learned few new things about Mercury over the next decade and a half. Then, in 1991, two scientists made important discoveries about Mercury's poles. John Harmon of the National Astronomy and Ionosphere Center in Arecibo, Puerto Rico, and Martin Slade of the Jet Propulsion Laboratory at the California Institute of Technology in Pasadena, California, independently discovered that Mercury's polar areas reflected strong radar signals. Scientists knew that, when other planets reflected these kinds of signals, ice was present. Yet people were baffled by the thought that ice could survive on the planet closest to the blazing Sun.

On March 24, 1974, Mariner 10 ▷ took its first image of Mercury. The spacecraft was 3.3 million miles (5.3 million kilometers) from the planet's surface.

Harmon compared the radar data with images of Mercury taken on the Mariner missions, and he realized that the strongest signals matched up with the positions of polar craters. The data also revealed that the floors of Mercury's polar craters never saw the Sun. Later studies showed that these areas could be as cold as −350°F (−213°C), which is easily cold enough for water-based ice to remain for billions of years. Although scientists have found that Mercury sometimes captures trace amounts of hydrogen and oxygen—both elements in water—the exact source of the polar ice is still a mystery. Some researchers have suggested that any ice is left over from collisions with comets.

▶ The *Messenger* Mission

Scientists hope that the clues needed to unlock Mercury's remaining mysteries will be found on the *Messenger* space mission. The unmanned spacecraft, launched August 3, 2004, will use a gravity assist from Venus, much like the *Mariner 10* craft did thirty years earlier. *Messenger* will perform flybys of Mercury in 2008 and 2009 and will enter Mercury's orbit in 2011. *Messenger*'s long journey will include fifteen loops around the Sun as well as one trip past Earth, two flybys of Venus, and three trips past Mercury. During the Mercury flybys, the spacecraft will map almost the entire planet in color—including most of the areas that were not captured by *Mariner 10*. In addition, *Messenger* will determine the composition of the planet's surface, core, atmosphere, and magnetic field. And, at long last, *Messenger* will shed light on the mysterious material—thought to be ice— that exists on the planet's poles.

Once *Messenger* goes into Mercury's orbit, it will conduct detailed research over the course of a twelve-month period. The spacecraft will investigate the Caloris Basin and other specific features. Occasionally, the spacecraft will perform course corrections to stay in orbit. Sunlight exerts a force on objects—called solar radiation pressure—that can gradually knock a small spacecraft off course.

"Mercury still stands out as a planet with a fascinating story to tell," said NASA official Orlando Figueroa. "*Messenger* should complete the detailed exploration of the inner solar system—our planetary backyard—and help us to understand the forces that shaped planets like our own."[1]

Messenger *orbits Mercury in this image created by an artist. During its year-long study of Mercury, the spacecraft will map the planet and determine its composition.*

Future Missions to Mercury

After *Messenger,* planetary researchers do not intend to wait thirty more years before the next mission to Mercury. The European Space Agency (ESA), in cooperation with the Japanese space agency ISAS/JAXA, is already planning its own Mercury mission, called *BepiColombo.* This cooperative mission was named in honor of Giuseppe "Bepi" Colombo, an Italian mathematician and engineer whose work on the *Mariner 10* mission was instrumental in the craft repeatedly reaching an orbit that brought it back to Mercury.

Scheduled to launch in 2012, the mission will arrive at Mercury more than three years later, braving temperatures as high as 482°F (250°C). It was to have featured the first-ever attempt

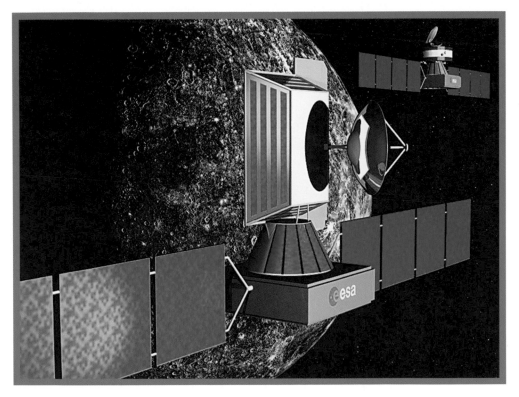

▲ *The European Space Agency is currently in the planning stages of the next mission to Mercury. This artist's drawing depicts the* BepiColombo *mission, which is scheduled to launch in 2012.*

The launch of Messenger *on its ▷ seven-year journey to Mercury.*

to land on Mercury, but the cost of building a lander became too great.

The mission will include two spacecraft. The Mercury Planetary Orbiter (MPO), built by the ESA, will gather information on the surface and composition of the planet. The Mercury Magnetosphere Orbiter (MMO), built by Japan, will study the region containing Mercury's magnetic field.

The scientists who are planning for this mission are excited by what they should be able to learn about the planet closest to the Sun. *BepiColombo* scientist Rita Schulz summed up the feelings of others who are eagerly awaiting the results of this Mercury mission.

> Mercury is extremely odd . . . We simply do not understand why it is like it is—but when we do, we will know not only so much more about how it was formed, but also about how our solar system was formed. Because it is so close to the Sun, Mercury

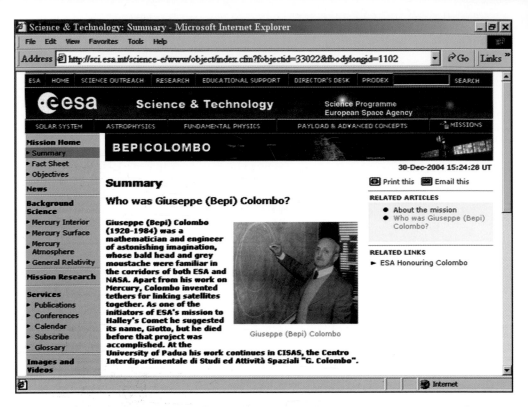

ESA   HOME   SCIENCE OUTREACH   RESEARCH   EDUCATIONAL SUPPORT   DIRECTOR'S DESK   PRODEX   SEARCH

●esa   Science & Technology

Science Programme
European Space Agency

SOLAR SYSTEM   ASTROPHYSICS   FUNDAMENTAL PHYSICS   PAYLOAD & ADVANCED CONCEPTS   ●⌐ MISSIONS

Mission Home
► Summary
► Fact Sheet
► Objectives

News

Background Science
► Mercury Interior
► Mercury Surface
► Mercury Atmosphere
► General Relativity

Mission Research

Services
► Publications
► Conferences
► Calendar
► Subscribe
► Glossary

Images and Videos

BEPICOLOMBO

30-Dec-2004 15:24:28 UT

🖨 Print this   ✉ Email this

Summary

Who was Giuseppe (Bepi) Colombo?

Giuseppe (Bepi) Colombo (1920-1984) was a mathematician and engineer of astonishing imagination, whose bald head and grey moustache were familiar in the corridors of both ESA and NASA. Apart from his work on Mercury, Colombo invented tethers for linking satellites together. As one of the initiators of ESA's mission to Halley's Comet he suggested its name, Giotto, but he died before that project was accomplished. At the University of Padua his work continues in CISAS, the Centro Interdipartimentale di Studi ed Attività Spaziali "G. Colombo".

Giuseppe (Bepi) Colombo

RELATED ARTICLES
● About the mission
● Who was Giuseppe (Bepi) Colombo?

RELATED LINKS
► ESA Honouring Colombo

⌂   🌐 Internet

▲ The European Space Agency has named its future mission to Mercury after Giuseppe "Bepi" Colombo, an Italian engineer and mathematician. Professor Colombo was instrumental in helping to guide the Mariner 10 spacecraft on its flybys of Mercury in the mid-1970s.

does pose enormous challenges for scientists hoping to get a closer look, especially since most instruments on Earth can be damaged just by looking in that direction. So many of our questions can only be answered by going there.[2]

Living up to its mythological name, Mercury may soon be sending us more messages about the origin of the solar system and its own mysterious history.

Glossary

albedo—The reflective power of a body, such as a planet.

asteroids—Rocky objects in space that can range greatly in size.

atmosphere—A layer (or layers) of gas that surrounds a planet or star.

attitude—A spacecraft's or aircraft's position that is determined by its relationship to another object, such as the horizon or a star.

comets—Frozen masses of gas and dust that have a definite orbit in our solar system.

ejecta blankets—Material ejected from, or thrown out of, craters. These spread out in rays or halos from the basin.

elliptical—Shaped like an oval; planetary orbits are elliptical rather than circular.

impact craters—Craters formed by the impact of a collision between a large body, such as a planet, and a smaller body, such as a meteor or a comet.

interstellar—Referring to the region in space between stars.

meteors—Fragments of material that fall from space.

molten—Melted.

scarps—Large cliffs that are parts of some highland regions.

Chapter 1. Mercury the Messenger

1. *The New York Times,* "NASA's Messenger Probe Departs for Mercury," August 3, 2004.

2. NASA press release, "NASA Sending a Messenger to Mercury," July 15, 2004, <www.nasa.gov/home/hqnews/2004/jul/HQ_04215 _mercury.html> (December 10, 2004).

Chapter 2. The First Planet From the Sun

1. J. Kelly Beatty et al., eds., *The New Solar System* (Cambridge, Mass.: Sky Publishing Corporation and Cambridge University Press, 1999), p. 96.

Chapter 3. Rotations and Revolutions

1. Robert Strom, *Mercury: The Elusive Planet* (Washington, D.C.: Smithsonian Institution Press, 1987), pp. 52, 54.

Chapter 4. Special Features

1. J. Kelly Beatty et al., eds., *The New Solar System* (Cambridge, Mass.: Sky Publishing Corporation and Cambridge University Press, 1999), p. 93.

2. Robert Strom, *Mercury: The Elusive Planet* (Washington, D.C.: Smithsonian Institution Press, 1987), p. 91.

Chapter 5. Exploring Mercury

1. NASA press release, "NASA Sending a Messenger to Mercury," July 15, 2004, <www.nasa.gov/home/hqnews/2004/jul/HQ_04215 _mercury.html> (December 10, 2004).

2. European Space Agency, "Mercury Rising: An Interview With Rita Schulz," September 17, 2003, <www.esa.int/export/esaSC/ SEMAQ10P4HD_index_0_iv.html> (December 10, 2004).

Further Reading

Asimov, Isaac, with revisions and updating by Richard Hantula. *Mercury.* Milwaukee: Gareth Stevens Publishing, 2002.

Cole, Michael D. *Mercury—The First Planet.* Berkeley Heights, N.J.: Enslow Publishers, Inc., 2001.

Croce, Carlo P. *Mercury.* New York: Rosen Publishing Group, 2004.

Kerrod, Robin. *Mercury and Venus.* Minneapolis: Lerner Publications, 2000.

Miller, Ron. *Mercury and Pluto.* Brookfield, Conn.: Twenty-First Century Books, 2003.

Nicolson, Cynthia Pratt. *Exploring Space.* Toronto: Kids Can Press, 2000.

Pasachoff, Jay A. *A Field Guide to the Stars and Planets.* Boston: Houghton Mifflin, 2000.

Ride, Sally, and Tam O'Shaughnessy. *Exploring Our Solar System.* New York: Crown Publishers, 2003.

Spangenburg, Ray, and Kit Moser. *A Look at Mercury.* New York: Franklin Watts, 2003.

Vogt, Gregory. *Mercury, Venus, Earth, and Mars.* Austin, Tex.: Steadwell Books, 2001.

A
albedo, 30
Arecibo observatory, 32
atmosphere, 12, 14, 21–22, 30, 40

B
Beethoven, 32
BepiColombo, 42–44

C
Colombo, Giuseppe "Bepi," 42, 44
color, 12, 40
composition, 12, 19, 40, 43
Copernicus, Nicolaus, 15

D
day, 22, 24
Denning, William, 11
density, 12, 19, 37
diameter, 12, 20, 23
Dickens, Charles, 32

E
ejecta blankets, 21
European Space Agency, 42–44

G
Galilei, Galileo, 11, 20
geography
    basins, 32–34, 40
    Caloris Basin, 29, 32–34, 40
    craters, 20–22, 29–30, 32, 35, 40
    highlands, 12, 29–30
    intercrater plains, 30
    Kuiper Quadrangle, 20
    lowlands, 12, 29–30
    Odin Formation, 34
    scarps, 29–30, 32
    Van Eyck Formation, 34
Goldstone observatory, 32
gravitational pull, 21

H
Halley, Edmond, 26–28
Harmon, John, 39–40
Harriot, Thomas, 11

I
ISAS/JAXA, 42

K
Kepler, Johannes, 15
Kuiper, Gerard P., 32

M
magnetic field, 14, 19, 37, 40, 43
maps, 11, 35, 37, 40–41
Mariner 10, 16, 19–20, 29, 31, 34–40, 42, 44
mass, 37
Mercury Magnetosphere Orbiter, 43
Mercury Planetary Orbiter, 43
Messenger, 12–14, 29, 40–43
Michelangelo, 32
mythology, 10–11, 13, 44

N
National Aeronautics and Space Administration (NASA), 11–12, 35, 37

O
orbit, 12, 19, 24, 26, 28, 40
origin, 17–18, 35, 44

P
polar ice caps, 22, 39–40
Ptolemy, 15

R
rotation, 19, 24, 26

S
Schiaparelli, Giovanni, 11
Slade, Martin, 39
solar radiation pressure, 40–41
spin-orbit coupling, 26
structure
    core, 14, 18–19, 40
    crust, 14, 18–19, 23, 32
    mantle, 18–19
surface, 11–12, 14, 18–20, 22–23, 30, 32, 37, 39–40, 43

T
temperature, 11, 21–23, 40, 42
transit, 26–28

V
Victoria, 32